AF255204

Don't Lose Your Joy

"In *Don't Lose Your Joy*, Stephen Ako-Nai takes us into the mystery of planting a seed of joy today as the promise of hope for tomorrow. It is a reminder of the important role of joy in a believer's journey of faith, perseverance, and maturity. In reading and sharing this book, you will be greatly blessed."

—ESTHER O. EDGAL, infection prevention specialist

"Embrace the transformative journey towards unshakeable joy through *Don't Lose Your Joy*. This practical guide illuminates the path to finding unwavering happiness amidst life's toughest trials, drawing strength from the boundless well of God's presence. Through poignant insights and actionable wisdom, this book is a beacon of hope for those seeking enduring joy. A must-read for anyone yearning to discover the true source of lasting joy."

—CHRIS OLHA, oncology sales and marketing specialist

"With infectious joy and unwavering faith, Stephen Ako-Nai inspires everyone he meets. For nearly twenty years, I've told my students about Stephen. Now, his story will encourage you, inspire you, and fill you with exuberance for life."

—AARON TITUS, professor of physics,
North Carolina State University

"Want to live a life of joy and integrity? This book is for you. To apply Stephen's eight declarations every morning in our lives will certainly bring us closer to God."

—JOE LENNA, chaplain

"*Don't Lose Your Joy* is a must-read. Steve shares his personal experience and identifies the source of joy, the truth, and the fountain of happiness, which I have come to know rests with our Lord and Savior Jesus Christ. 'Thou wilt shew me the path of life: in thy presence is fullness of joy; at thy right hand there are pleasures for evermore' (Ps 16:11 KJV)."

—ELI AYOUB, vice president, Specialty Pharmacy

Don't Lose Your Joy

STEPHEN AKO-NAI

Foreword by David B. Crabtree

RESOURCE *Publications* · Eugene, Oregon

DON'T LOSE YOUR JOY

Resource Publications
An Imprint of Wipf and Stock Publishers
199 W. 8th Ave., Suite 3
Eugene, OR 97401

www.wipfandstock.com

PAPERBACK ISBN: 978-1-6667-8520-3
HARDCOVER ISBN: 978-1-6667-8521-0
EBOOK ISBN: 978-1-6667-8522-7

This book is humbly dedicated to my beautiful wife, Harriet, for her selfless love, our four incredible kids, Caleb, Michaela, Joshua, and Madison, for their commitments to family values, and to all inmates throughout the world for their persistent hope of improving themselves.

Contents

Foreword by David B. Crabtree ix

Preface xiii

1 The seed of joy 1

2 Your joy is your strength 6

3 Miracles of laughter 14

4 Life's journey 19

5 It's never too late to start again 24

6 From prison to prominence 33

7 Character creates champions 40

8 Life is short, live 46

9 Your word is your world 55

About the Author 59

Foreword

In the forty-two years I have served in a preaching ministry the people who have crossed my path would number in the thousands. Notable among them is Stephen Ako-Nai, a dedicated husband and father, a devoted pharmacist, a minister to prisoners, a generous friend, a faithful parishioner . . . my parishioner. His family cannot cross my mind without a smile breaking out on my face and in my soul.

Stephen was unique in a number of ways, having come to our shores from Ghana, having suffered life-threatening tragedies, having sacrificed deeply to acquire a rich education, and having engaged in outreach almost from the first day he stepped through the doors of Calvary Church. He also possessed a smile that was easy, constant, welcoming, and contagious. I wasn't surprised when I saw the title Stephen chose for his book. Stephen Ako-Nai is a joyful man, and if you'll read the following chapters you'll understand why.

I remember reading *You Gotta Keep Dancing* by Tim Hansel in the early years of my ministry. Tim wrote of the necessity of choosing joy. I had never really thought of joy as a choice. Tim was a man who lived in constant pain from a tragic accident, and yet Tim refused to play the victim. He made a compelling case for choosing joy. Stephen carries that same torch from a different life experience. Victor Frankl famously said, "Everything can be taken from a man but one thing: the last of the human freedoms—to choose one's attitude in any given set of circumstances, to choose one's own way." Frankl made a philosophical point. Stephen

Ako-Nai makes a theological point. God created us with an incredible capacity for joy.

Stephen talks about joy as seed, not as the result of the things that happen to us or the things that happen around us. He challenges us to recognize that we have the opportunity—even the responsibility—to plant the seeds of joy in everything we do and to expect a harvest of righteousness. I watched Stephen live this out to the fullest in his life of service and in his family. He raises a very challenging statement: "If you can be angry and lose your joy, then you can be joyful and lose your anger!" In our angry world we look for outside forces to bring joy and happiness to our tumultuous circumstances. Stephen doesn't look to the horizon for a happenstance deliverer, he looks to the seeds of joy that can be sown in the midst of the storm (even seed sown in a storm will produce a harvest). We need to be reminded that we shouldn't wait for the ship to come in that has never been sent out.

Stephen has had what many would consider ample reasons to be bitter with life, but he decided early on that he would never let anyone take his joy. He treasures this seed and sows generously. He writes a whole chapter on laughter as a medicine. You should pay attention; after all, Stephen is a pharmacist. "LOL" is an acronym for "laughing out loud." Our social media, texts, and emails are littered with that tired expression and its yellow emoji. If only we did laugh out loud so much as we claim, the world would be a brighter place. Stephen writes, "Your joy is your strength. Lose your joy and you will lose your strength." Stories abound of athletes who channeled some inner rage to a high level of performance, but great performance isn't life. The trophy moment passes and the rage remains. Joy, on the other hand, yields a boundless harvest. Joy is a greater motivator.

Stephen lays the responsibility for joy at our doorstep. We can't look without; we need to look within. He fills his chapters with biblical illustration, not as one who is looking for sure up a point, but as one who has found biblical models and mentors for his own journey. Stephen chooses the good company of Joseph, Moses, David, and Namaan's heroic servant girl. He takes us to the wisdom of Psalms and Proverbs. He challenges us to live with character and purpose. He calls us to live by faith and speak biblically to a world devoid of love. He isn't presenting an ideal or promoting a novel theory. Stephen has tested and tried cultivating joy and found something well worth sharing with the world. It's bigger than his smile!

David B. Crabtree
Assistant Superintendent/Secretary NCAG
Raleigh, NC

Preface

The power of maintaining your joy is an essential guide for anyone looking to overcome anger, create positive perception, and achieve their purpose in life. Through a combination of biblical guidance and practical advice, readers will explore the nature of joy and the need to master joy to live a more fulfilling life.

In this book, I will share my life story and incorporate lessons learned about joy, tragedy, and anger. We are all created to enjoy life, not to endure, whether we realize it or not. Our daily routines and habits shape our lives, determining how successful we are likely to be in our personal and professional lives. Habits of joy can be cultivated with the right approach. We will examine the power of routines, the benefits of positive reinforcement, and the importance of setting smart, achievable goals. Readers will walk away with the tools and knowledge they need to create lasting positive change in their lives.

Readers will learn how to form habits of joy, why they are so important to cultivate, and how they affect our behaviors daily. Readers will gain a better understanding of their joy; learn why they behave the way they do; break unhealthy habits of anger; explore strategies for overcoming anger, procrastination, other harmful habits; and learn how to replace negative angers with positive joys to transform their lives.

1

The seed of joy

Planting a seed of joy today is the promise of hope for your tomorrow.

A SEED IS ANYTHING that has the potential for growth. When you sow a seed, you begin to anticipate its fruits soon. Although the fruits might not be immediate, you still believe that since the seed is planted, the fruit of its kind will show up at the appropriate time. Life is about seeds and fruits; it's about sowing and reaping. For instance, you invest money to reap more than what was invested, sow or put in more hours at work to receive a salary matching your input. You sow or spend much time with your wife, husband, children, or loved ones to enrich these relationships. I could go on to mention many more examples to prove that life is about sowing and reaping, but in short, where you are today is because of the type of seed you planted yesterday.

The origin of life started with the principle of sowing and reaping. God could have, for he has the power to put all eight billion people on earth at once, but he did not. Instead, he created Adam and Eve to reproduce, multiply, and replenish the earth. Then when God drew his redemption plan, he did not save the entire world at once. Instead, he planted his only begotten son, Jesus Christ, to die for our sins so that anyone who believes in him shall be saved and not perish. Now that you have an idea of what I mean by the principle of sowing and reaping, let us go ahead to look at some attributes or properties of a seed. Anything that grows or multiplies can be traced to its source, or its seed. When you invest money, you reap multiple benefits. When you sow just a single corn seed, you reap multiple benefits of it. When you sow your time to work Mondays to Fridays from 8 a.m. to 5 p.m., you receive a check at the end of the week. You see, everything you do in life can be traced to sowing and reaping. Consider this: if you spend time praying and studying the Scriptures every day, then you are giving God your time. He responds by having fellowship with you. If this is true for you, you leave your home to go to work or school filled with enthusiasm and a positive mindset to confront your day after such inspiring fellowship.

Time is extremely sensitive to the seed of joy. You pay much attention to the things that are important to you. A shepherd spends much time with his sheep. An author spends much time writing. You spend a lot of time on the things you love doing. When God created you, he planted in you both the seed of joy and anger, but you gravitate toward the one you spend time feeding and nurturing. It is your choice to nurture the seed of your joy or anger and reap the corresponding effect. Nurture anger and you will reap multitudes of strife, hatred, hurt, bitterness, unfulfilled life, and a list of other undesirable emotions that anger fuels. Nurture the seed of joy and you will reap droves of peace, love, influence, positive countenance, happiness, and a purposeful and fulfilled life.

It can easily be deduced that you reap what you sow. You can only reap fruit after you have planted a seed, and you will reap multiples of your seed type. Joy is a wonderful seed when cultivated and nurtured in its source; that source is God. It is in your inner man. I must say that nurturing your joy is not passive but active. You nurture your joy by consistently involving your thinking to see the little positive things in everything you go through in life, whether good or bad.

This is not an easy task, but deliberate effort, consistency, and perseverance will make it possible. Let us look at a scripture from Ps 126:6: *"Those who go out weeping, carrying seed to sow, will return with songs of joy, carrying sheaves with them."* The Bible affirms that sowing a seed is difficult yet possible. You see, nothing on earth can be achieved without some amount of effort. You just have to look beyond the pain and torture that precedes the fruits bore from planting lasting seeds of joy. Let me demonstrate the realities a seed may go through to become a plant and give off its fruits.

The mustard seed is the tiniest seed, but when planted it grows to become one of the strongest trees with huge branches that provide glorious shade for you and me to relax beneath. If this strong tree should have a mouth to speak for itself, I believe it would tell you how tiny it was when planted into the ground. I believe it would state that it was difficult to break through the soil. Also, after breaking through it would reminisce on the difficulty to start protruding through the ground. I imagine this tree would tell tales of how people trampled on it, animals fed on it, and heavy wind blew against it to break it. Sometimes the sun might have been too hot and sometimes the rainfall too heavy, yet through it all, all these debilitating factors made it stronger to survive and become what it was destined to be—a mighty tree.

While nurturing your joy you may have to go through similar processes. You do not have to focus on the pain it brings to you today, but rather focus on the pleasant fruits it will reciprocate tomorrow. Remember, the Bible asserts, *"those who sow with tears will reap with songs of joy"* (Ps 126:5). Joy is precious, and anything that is precious demands maximum attention and protection. As you protect and develop your joy, you may encounter some devastating obstacles that are enough to cause you to shed tears. But that is okay; in fact, it is part of the process. During moments of sorrow, remain strong-minded and never lose your joy. Keep in mind that the strength and height any tree can attain is determined by how deep its root has penetrated the ground. The same is true for joy. The energy and time you devote today will determine your blessings tomorrow. You will have uncommon joy as you respond positively to undesirable situations.

When you sow a seed, it does not give you immediate returns. You must keep tending to it. For example, an apple seed does not take a day to grow. But with time, water, and sunlight, apples will sprout. The germination process takes about five to seven years, but if you take on the responsibility to actively nurture that seed, the plant will grow and bear delicious fruit. The beginning might be a challenge for the apple seed to break forth through fallow ground, and the same principle is applied to the seed of joy. It might take years to develop and equilibrate your joy; you may not see the outcome immediately, but you must keep developing it actively and consciously. This same joy you are developing today, without giving you any immediate response, will definitely take care of you tomorrow after it has been fully established. One sign that will be evident in the process of developing your joy is that the things that easily make you angry will no longer easily irritate you; instead, you will find yourself in a resourceful state to handle such situations.

Remember that there are three things you can do to your seed of joy. You can trade it, consume it, or sow it. When you get angry at something, your anger is sustained by the memories of whatever situations that might have led to that feeling, and the more you think about those situations, the more you slowly but surely trade your joy for anger. When you get aggravated and lose or trade your joy it is because you ponder over those situations, and your mind justifies your anger. You cannot trade for anything you do not have. This is to say that you are capable of showing evidence of joy and anger.

If you can be angry and lose your joy, then you can be joyful and lose your anger.

You can also choose to consume your joy. But if you consume your joy today, you do not have a tomorrow. Your joy is inversely proportional to your anger; you either have more of one and less or neither of the other. Some people are so angry that they do not see anything pleasing and joyful. You do not have to be a millionaire to be joyful. Take some time to enjoy the little things around you such as your family, friends and the life God has granted you today. You only have one life to live, so plant and develop your joy by finding joy in even the most trivial situations. By doing this consciously, you will unconsciously find yourself in a peaceful state with time, and at this state you will have tons of reasons to be joyful when others do not see anything exciting. Life is a gift, and any gift must be first accepted and enjoyed in its totality, so enjoy your life.

The third action one may take with a seed is to plant it. One factor to consider before sowing a seed is the type of soil you will be sowing into. Whether or not a seed will germinate and flourish is mostly dependent on where it is planted. According to Jer 4:3, *"This is what the Lord says to the people of Judah and to Jerusalem: Break up your unplowed ground and do not sow among thorns."* Is your joy based on smoking a pack of cigarettes a day or getting drunk? Is it based on temporarily getting high with marijuana or other drugs? If these are the basis of your joy, then I am afraid to tell you that you are planting your joy in tainted soil. Those bases are short term and are like thorns that will eventually pierce or backfire on you. Instead, plant your joy based on God's word. Such joy will be pleasant and lasting, since God is immutable and so is his word. If the source of your joy is God, your strength will not fail in times of harsh conditions.

2

Your joy is your strength

*Your joy is your strength. Lose your joy
and you will lose your strength*

YOUR STRENGTH IS THE energy or influence you can exert when confronted with circumstances. Confronting your circumstances successfully is dependent on whether you are in a resourceful state or not. Your resourceful state is yet again determined by the state of your joy. If you are joyful and pleased with your life, then you will have the strength and courage to conquer your confrontations.

Life is full of inexplicable variables and will not always offer us what we really wanted. So, if we cannot predict what tomorrow might bring our way, we can at least prepare for tomorrow no matter what it offers. This is to say that you must always do the best you can to be in a resourceful state, ready for life. When the state of your joy is perturbed, your strength is threatened. According to the Bible, Nehemiah had a good connection between joy and strength. In Neh 8:10, Nehemiah said, *"Go and enjoy choice food and sweet drinks, and send some to those who have nothing prepared. This day is holy to our Lord. Do not grieve, for the joy of the LORD is your strength."* If your joy is your strength, then conversely your anger is your weakness. If you take anything from this book, please get this: do not let anybody take away your joy. The only way your enemy can knock you out is to steal your joy and make you feeble. I would give you a biblical account of a scenario where this strategy was applied and its application in our contemporary world.

Any time the Philistines drew near to fight against the Israelites, Goliath, the giant, would always go ahead of the Philistines and verbally insult the Israelites. For instance, he would use demeaning words to defy the armies of Israel each day. This type of strategy of the enemy is what I am trying to make you aware of so you can recognize and guard against it. Listen; so long as Goliath verbally intimidated the armies of Israel, the Israelites lost the joy of memories of the past victories God had brought them against their enemies. They became dismayed and were gripped with fear, making them vulnerable to the Philistines. The Philistines continued to intimidate the Israelites until David, a shepherd boy, who understood the principles of joy and strength, challenged him. David applied the same strategy Goliath was using against the armies of Israel to defeat Goliath. On the battlefield, David also challenged Goliath by using demeaning words. For example, David said, "Who is this uncircumcised Philistine [Goliath] to defy the armies of the living God, for this day the Lord will deliver you into my hands and will cut you into pieces to feed the birds of the air." As Goliath heard such words from the mouth of a small shepherd boy, he became angry, light, and eventually lost his balance and became vulnerable to David's sling. *Anger will make you lighter and imbalanced.*

Another example, in our contemporary world: Muhammad Ali was a great boxer who used his understanding of joy and strength to his advantage in the ring. Only five of Muhammad Ali's sixty-one fights ended in defeat. Ali used ridiculous tactics in the ring. As part of these strategies, Ali verbally insulted and intimidated his opponents. As a result, the opponents became enraged at his words, and as they concentrated on those demeaning words, they became angrier, lighter, and eventually lost their balance. At this point, if they tried to hit Ali but failed, they would fall to the ground, and if Ali hit them, they would also fall to the ground. When he attacks you and me, the devil employs the same tactic: He will put pressure on your mind and make you feel like a failure. He will frequently express negative emotions, such as you are a failure, you will never be able to pay off your debt, you will become like your alcoholic father, and you will not be worth anything because you are poor, a woman, uneducated, overweight, and ugly. None of these ideas will help you. Instead, if you paid attention to those demeaning words, you would be enraged not only at yourself but also at other innocent people in your life. Friends, there is one thing you can always do instead of being bitter: decide NOT TO LOSE YOUR JOY every morning you wake up and do very much like what Bob Marley said in his song: "wake up in the morning and smile with the rising sun." If you are going to have a successful day, you must strengthen yourself each morning by waking up with a grateful heart and speaking positively to yourself and making declaration that gives you favor before God and your fellowmen. For me, every morning, I intentionally and meaningfully declare the following:

1. This is the day the Lord has made for me.

2. I choose to be happy among unhappy people.

3. I choose to smile at those that frown at me.

4. I choose to love those that hate me.

5. I choose to be there for those that will never be there for me.

6. I choose to make someone's life better than I met it.

7. I choose to be me and not anybody else.

8. So, help me God.

As I become mindful of those declarations, I am able to position myself in a resourceful state to better handle situations that are either negative or positive. This is because everyday experience is probably applicable to one of those statements and constrains me to act accordingly for a better outcome, and also helps me think in the right direction.

The only difference between the thoughts you are entertaining now and the actions you will be executing later is the unspoken word. For instance, if one wants to figure out what you are thinking, all one must do is observe your behavior. This is because your behavior is the acting out of your thoughts. Remember the Bible says that "as a man thinketh so is he" (Prov 23:6 KJV). You are what you think. Any behavior you exhibit at any point in time is a result of your thought process at that moment. So, you actually communicate to yourself by the kinds of thoughts you entertain in your mind. For this reason, be extraordinarily strong in your mind and constantly remind yourself not to lose that beautiful joy, no matter what you go through in life.

No one can take away your joy without your approval.

Some people have become so vulnerable to their critics in such a way that their critics know exactly when and which button to press to ignite their anger. Such people can easily be predicted at any point in life since their approval of such buttons always results in losing their joy. If your enemy can make you lose your joy, then he stands a better chance of defeating you. This is because losing your joy in moments of adversities will result in anger, which is the weakest unreliable weapon one can use. If someone should hurt or make you angry, how do you know you are hurt? You know you are hurt because you felt you were right, and the person was wrong. But if you can pause for a moment to see things from the other person's perspective, sensitive matters can be resolved amicably without leaving any scar on you. Life is not about who is right and who is wrong. It is about how we live and enjoy moments together even in the presence of our differences. The only difference between you and the person who might have hurt you is that the person acted differently from what you expected. I strongly believe that our bodies demand more energy out of us to be angry than to be joyful. So do not allow anybody to take away your joy, and for that matter your strength. This is because the level of your strength when hard-pressed in every sphere of your life will determine who you are at that time in life. In tough times, it is extremely easy for people to lose their joy because of numerous circumstances that might be demanding their attention. Your spouse, child, or family member might be demanding your attention. Your boss at work and the bills in your mailbox are demanding your attention as well. All these factors have the potential to build you or destroy you depending on how you appropriately decide to handle them in a way that will bring you joy rather than anger.

Growing up in Ghana can be challenging enough, but losing both parents can present significant difficulties with multiple financial struggles, emotional, and educational challenges. Even in developing nations like Ghana, government assistance is scarce and often difficult to obtain. As a result, people like me who have lost both of their parents frequently find themselves without any means of support. This can make it hard to pay for things like food and a place to live, as well as make it hard to get into education or job training programs that could help people get out of poverty. I lost my mother when I was a teenager. My mother was all I had ever known or needed at that time as I enjoyed her provisions and tender loving care. When my father assumed full responsibility of my life after my mother's death, he also died about a year or so after my mother's death. Thus, I lost two valuable personalities in my life within a short period of time. As my dying father struggled to communicate with my elder brother at the hospital, knowing that his time was limited and that he had so much he wanted to say to his children, as he lay dying and his breaths were coming to short breaths, he told my brother, "Tell Stephen not to be distracted by women, and that he should go the highest he can on the academic ladder." As my brother told me my father's final words before he died, I nodded my head in sorrow and said in a choked voice that I would determine to succeed academically to make my parents proud. I have worked extremely hard over the years, studying and never forgetting my dying father's final words, and I have eventually advanced in education and earned a doctorate degree in pharmacy. I felt their presence in every achievement, and every moment of life, even though my parents were no longer with me. The loss of both parents brought on a wide range of feelings, including grief and anxiety. These feelings were intense for me as I was developing my sense of identity and the place of my role in the world, and it was hard to find solid ways of adapting to these feelings without parental help. Another significant obstacle that I faced was the difficulty of my education. It can be hard to get an education and even harder to stay in school if parents don't provide financial support and direction. At that time, many Ghanaians around my age can be forced to drop out of school to work and support themselves, making it even more difficult for them to break the poverty cycle and build a better future. All hope was gone, and the only one I could think of having the funds to take care of me was my elder brother. My senior brother took me and really focused on me as one of his kids. He gave me everything I needed to do well in high school. Within a similar time span to my dad, I lost my senior brother as well. I was extremely worried and afraid of life at this point, I went to my senior sister who by then possessed the ability to support me. She was so terrified to take care of me and said something that was so frightening to the extent that I felt I had tasted life's most awful offer. She said everybody that attempts to take care of you bites the dust. She assumed that if she took on the responsibility of taking care of me, she would soon die. I left her presence with tears dripping down my cheeks as I vowed to intercede and pleaded with God to stop this accelerated pattern of death in my family. As some of my siblings stood the same ground with me and interceded in that direction, the pattern of death was broken. I'm still alive, and no death has been reported in the family from that point onward. If you've ever been in a similar predicament, you might be thinking, that's your lot in life because no one in your family has lived more than forty years, married more than five years, or had children. Don't accept that; it's your turn to break the cycle and free your generation and the next from this shackle. I frequently pondered the unfairness of it. I strolled across the roads of Ghana and individuals pointed fingers at me, feeling for me, and making statements like, "I feel sorry for this boy because he did not get a good start in life. What else could have happened to him?" It goes on and on. However, during all of these trying times, my faith in God steadily increased while my trust in people dramatically decreased. I began spending more time in prayer, studying and memorizing scriptures in the Bible, and eventually turned out to be completely convinced that if I could stay in the environment of God's word, God would take me to places I never dreamt of. I made a major decision that I would never let tragedy or the loss of all the people I trusted with my life take away my joy. Those people once existed and left their footprints on our planet; however, their genes have been removed from the planet's surface and their footprints have been erased forever. Therefore, do not put your faith in any man because they might disappoint you; instead, put your faith in God and you will soar like an eagle. The joy of being in the Lord brought hope to me and gave me every reason to have a good success in all my endeavors. Today, I am where I am because I took time to nurture that joy that comes from within. People can rob you of your money, tell lies about you, strip you of your clothes and put you in jail, but they cannot take away your joy.

In your darkest moment is your greatest opportunity to shine.

When the road of life becomes dark with unexpected tribulations, disappointments, or life-threatening illness, the easiest thing one can do is to give up and say that he or she is done in life and cannot see through the dark anymore. This is not the time to give up, it is your opportunity to encourage yourself in the Lord and show the world that you can still be positive and enjoy life even in your negative situation. The stars in the sky shine the brightest in the darkest night. The darkness only comes to reveal the beauty of those stars. Life really does work in hopeless circumstances when one decides to be positive and hopeful to survive. The darkest moments of your life shall also come to pass. It will not be dark forever in your life. Psalm 30:5 declares, *"Weeping may stay for the night, but rejoicing comes in the morning."* God wants you to enjoy life rather than endure life. Your moments of weeping, outrage, feelings of hatred, and the likes just come around evening time, but joy comes in the morning. Even though we are all human, we all get angry at some point in our lives, but staying angry for a long time is bad for our health. The night does not last for long, and so must be your anger. To prolong your joy, constantly feed it. In the first part of the day, the sun ascends to activate your expectation for the afternoon. For that reason, it is important to wake up with joy, and you will have the strength expected to fulfill your day. Running a race while carrying a lot of garbage is like going through life with anger. It slows you down and prevents you from achieving your goals. Like garbage, anger will slow you down, making it impossible to act appropriately and promptly. It is up to you whether to lose this energy or joy because some people are always happy to ensure that they make your life miserable by sucking happiness out of your atmosphere. Although you have no choice over a few things in life such as choosing who your mother or father should be, country of origin, gender, or race. You have choices over many things such as who to marry, being joyful or angry, where to live, who to be your friend, and the list goes on. The only difference between your today and tomorrow is simply the state of your joy. Some of you are in devastating situations that have robbed you of your strength and left you weak, ready to admit defeat. But if you can get back your joy, you can restore your strength, put the puzzle pieces of your life together, and have a good success because you are only a joy away from your success.

3

Miracles of laughter

Laugh daily even if you don't feel like it until your laughter becomes real and you laugh unconsciously.

THE BOOK OF PROV 17:22 states that *"a cheerful heart is good medicine, but a crushed spirit dries up the bones"* (NIV). Who wants good medicine, one may ask? Or better put, who wants to live a healthy lifestyle? I guess the answer of the majority will be the need for good medicine with minimum or no side effects. That is right. In our present-day world, medicine is awfully expensive and almost unaffordable among average class citizens. As expensive as prescription drugs are, I want to prescribe the most affordable drug for you. This prescription drug *is LAUGHTER*. Laughter is a good medicine without any side effects, yet it is free of charge. It is a fact that anybody anywhere at any time can afford laughter regardless of age, gender, or race. For instance, when babies are in their mothers' wombs, their lives are sustained by their mothers'. But the moment a baby exits a mother's womb, he or she automatically becomes self-sustained and begins to develop some characteristics that enable a baby's survival. Nobody taught those babies how to laugh, but a few weeks after their birth they naturally begin to smile and laugh. This should tell you that you were born with nature's medicine that constantly nourishes you upon release. You can benefit from this good medication that costs you nothing but a decision, especially in moments when the prices of prescription drugs are so high.

You may be raised or nurtured in a family that is too busy to laugh but try and develop or look for opportunities that will make you laugh very often. I heard about an Italian who grew up in a family that laughs a lot. This Italian had an uncle who laughs and really does laugh loud. This uncle was seriously disabled at birth but lived his life beyond his doctor's expectation. He was not expected to live past his fortieth birthday. It just happened that this uncle would laugh and laugh so loud and very often that he lived past his eightieth birthday and was still laughing out loud. If you have lost your laughter for any reason, please uncover it again since it can cost you more not to laugh than to laugh. Go back for your laughter and put that wonderful smile on your face again because you are destined to look and feel good after a good hearty laugh daily.

When a person is depressed or stressed out, one of the most prescribed drugs for such a depressed individual is a tranquilizer to minimize anxiety. Tranquilizers target the central nervous system to have their calming effects; this may result in a situation where one may become dependent or addicted to this sedating class of drugs. When you are too busy to laugh, you become so tense and serious with life that you tend to make big deals out of things that are no big deal at all. This is when depression gradually begins to work its way into your life as you fail to take some moments to relax, slow down, and laugh over things. Laughing will not cost you a penny, and as you laugh heartily, your body releases natural tranquilizers necessary to calm you and expedite the rate at which you become capable of making intelligent decisions in your day-to-day transactions.

When the right conditions are met, results are inevitable.

For water to boil at one hundred degrees Celsius, certain conditions must be right or met. Thus, under normal conditions, water will not boil until the vapor pressure of the water becomes equal to the atmospheric pressure. This is to say that things do not just happen; something must be done to cause something to happen. When you easily and frequently get angry at people, and you sit down all days, months, or years without changing your attitude, then nothing will change, and your anger will continue to grow from bad to worse. Can you imagine how unbearable life may be if all you do is to eat and you are not able to empty your bowels, or drink and not able to urinate. Then your organs will explode with all kinds of infections that will not be able to sustain your life. Thus, in life, there must be balances. Your inputs must balance your outputs.

God in his own infinite wisdom has designed us with the expression of laughter to bring some sense of balance in moments of anger. If you keep getting angrier and angrier without any outlet to release or unleash your anger, the inevitable result is an explosion. Laughter is one of the outlets to let go of your anger. We live in a world where we are always surrounded or intermingled with people all the time. These people are our friends, children, spouses, family members, neighbors, or strangers, and they are not perfect, and neither are we. But if we can smile with them and laugh together, then we can live together and have a sense of good feelings about ourselves and the people around us.

Most often people make the mistake of thinking that they will be happy when they get married and be able to have a good hearty laugh when they get that job and are in good health. No, they got it all wrong. You already have everything needed to make yourself happy and laugh heartily at your circumstances. Petty things in life such as breathing, eating for energy, and drinking for hydration are the driving force of life, and are basic to all humankind. For example, if your vision is to go to Florida or become a medical doctor, you do not close your eyes and suddenly get to Florida or become a medical doctor. Rather, you need to plan your trip by deciding how to get to Florida for instance. Do you want to go by flight, train, or car? After deciding your means of transportation, you need to start at rest (zero distance covered) to cover a distance less than a mile, then a mile, and continue to cover two miles, three miles, etc. to get to your destination. The distances covered before reaching your destination are built on each other and never isolated. This implies that your first mile covered is as important as your mid and final mile. Also, consider a stone breaker as another example. A stone breaker continues to strike the stone with his hammer several times until the stone is broken. Should the stone be broken by the twentieth strike of his hammer, it is not the twentieth strike alone that broke the stone, but all the previous strikes that went in to weaken the bonds within the stone. A hearty laugh is not the only way to be healthy and balance your anger, but it is as important as other health factors and the avoidance of circumstances that trigger your anger.

If you can laugh heartily and frequently at situations that are most stressful to you, you can be assured victory over those stressful circumstances rather than becoming a victim. Stressful moments can increase your blood pressure, but laughing can help lower it. The person who can pause in stressful moments to laugh can have a reason not to stress out and respond positively and efficiently to those circumstances without any bitterness. We cannot change what happens to us, but we can change how we respond. Psalm 2:4 declares, *"The One enthroned in Heaven laughs; the Lord scoffs at them."* The one seated in heaven refers to God Almighty. God, the creator of all things laughs to demonstrate the importance of laughter. When God laugh, he laughs at "them." Who are "them"? "Them" refers to our enemies, failures, obstacles, stressful moments, gossip and plots against us. God expects us to emulate his sense of humor and make fun of those situations. As you are making fun of those situations, you are strategically positioning yourself for God's best to conquer your confrontations. Couples that can laugh together can live together. Some of you are on the verge of losing your husband or wife. You are afraid of divorce, and about to give up thinking nothing else can save your marriage. Hold on; try one more ingredient of life's recipe: laughter. Get a comedy to watch together or something that can create an atmosphere of laughter or sense of humor in your home, and you will be amazed at the outcome. Whilst anger separates us from each other, laughter will bind us together in moments of trouble. So, laugh, and laugh out loud because someone else may need that laughter to brighten his or her day.

4

Life's Journey

A journey not defined is a destination never arrived.

LIFE IS A JOURNEY, and every journey leads to a destination. The journey of life is loaded with decisions, and those decisions are made by the traveler. You are the driving force behind your life's journey and determine your course. As you travel through life, you can find yourself on the road of joy or the road of rage. If you are already on the road of rage, you must turn around to return to the road of joy. The word "joy" spelled backwards is "YOJ (Your Own Journey)." If you do something that takes away your joy, turn around completely and do the opposite to regain it. Joy, as previously stated, is a journey that you actively control or dictate. There are a lot of rules to follow when going on a trip to make it safer, but here are a few that will almost always be followed, whether you are aware of them or not. First is the principle of a clearly defined destination, followed by the principles of departure, obstacles, decision-making, and arrival. Following is a discussion of each of these.

No other person can make you cheerful or joyous but you. It is up to you, and you alone, to decide if the joy journey is worth pursuing, and if you decide to embark on such a journey the first thing you do is to define your destination. Destination is the predetermined end of a journey. You will not even think about going on a trip until you have decided where you want to go. To put it simply, you never begin a journey until you have first determined where you want to end up. Your departure time, any potential street signs you may encounter, potential obstacles that could prevent you from reaching your destination, and well-informed decisions that would determine the success of your journey are all located between your specified destination and your proposed arrival. A flight plan must be filed by the pilot prior to takeoff. Destination, estimated arrival time, route, and departure time are all included in this flight plan. The ground crew can monitor and provide expert information on the pilot's and the crew's best interests based on the submitted flight plan, which serves as a guide for the pilot throughout the flight. The ground crew can locate the flight and carry out a rescue plan in accordance with the flight plan the pilot submitted if something goes wrong. Without a flight plan, a pilot circles around without reaching their destination. In a comparable manner, if you do not have a strategy for where you want to be at a specific time, you will be thrown anywhere at any time and will be doing things that will only lead you astray. Your destination predicts your arrival time, and your arrival time is influenced by the behavioral choices you make throughout the journey. For instance, the choices you make in situations that are likely to arouse your rage have a significant impact on how quickly you work through your anger. You must be determined and mentally strong to never allow yourself to be easily upset by insignificant issues if you want to work on your anger and turn it into joy. What do you do when you find yourself in an unexpected circumstance? Anything you search for or focus on in that situation would decide the result of such a circumstance. You will have concrete reasons to be upset if you go looking for them. On the other hand, if you look for a reason to be happy or joyful, you will once more discover exceptional reasons to be happy. It is amazing that while driving a car, you do not pay much attention to the various kinds of cars you see. However, when you purchase another vehicle like a red Toyota Camry, for instance, all you see around you are individuals driving a red Toyota Camry or a comparative vehicle recently bought. Does it imply that while you were driving your Honda Accord or Nissan Maxima, there were no red Toyota Camrys on the road? Definitely no, there are Hondas and Nissans surrounding you but since you are obsessed with your Camry and have centered such a great amount of attention around it all you see around you are vehicles of your kind. That is what attention can accomplish. You tend to see and meet people who have goals that are similar to yours when you define your destination and concentrate on what it takes to get there. This limits you to things that are relevant to your destination. Defining where you need to be at a specific point in life would eliminate unnecessary detours and interferences that might delay your arrival.

You must estimate the day and time of your departure when planning a trip because if you do not leave your current location, you will not get to your destination. Because nothing can be accomplished without effort, it is all about you making a move. Do not waste another second once you decide to work on your circumstances. You may be thinking and giving yourself excuses that the timing is not correct; however, I will say the timing is correct. No matter how insignificant it may be, get started right away. Similar to riding a bicycle, it will be extremely challenging for you to maintain your balance when the bike comes to a stop, regardless of how skilled you are. However, if the bicycle is moving, you will be able to control it in any direction. Get up and begin taking care of your circumstance, and as you make a specific move, roll out important improvements en route till you get to where you should have been. Even if things in your life are not perfect right now, keep working on them and making those informed decisions and you'll never fall into the syndrome of complacency mentality. There might be obstacles along the way and, yes, I guarantee there will be. However, there are street signs as well, guiding you all the way to your destination. For me, the obstacles were so tough to such an extent that they nearly shattered my dream, and you will say that's not a big deal. You are right; wait until your turn to sit in the front row and mourn your mother's death; wait until your turn to stand by your father's grave and watch the priest lay the first sand on his coffin, saying "dust to dust, naked you came to this earth, and naked will you depart this earth"; wait until your turn on the front row to be called out of the classroom and asked to leave because your tuition has not been paid. Through it all, I emerged out stronger because I paid attention to the signs around me, adhered to biblical principles, and followed the advice of friends and family. Your street signs are the people in your life with whom you interact daily and the choices you make based on your belief system. Some of the guidance may come as you read the Bible, pray, or hear an inspiring comment from a family member, friend, or coworker that awakens your awareness. Don't take these for granted, rather work with them to make decisions that are in line with your plans. Follow through on them until you achieve your goal. After all, no one can guarantee that life will be easy, so it's better to make a decision and stick with it even if it means failing than to not make any decision at all and regret it for the rest of your life while lying on your deathbed. Your past may have been difficult but put it behind you and have the courage to decide to go on and accomplish something, even when you are afraid. Even if you don't have all the answers right now, that shouldn't stop you from making a decision right away. When I decided to further my education in Massachusetts, I didn't have all the answers yet discussed with my lovely wife Harriet who supported my decision. We didn't know anyone in Massachusetts, and we hadn't been there before. However, after gaining admission to the pharmacy program, my wife and I made the decision to empty our apartment and donate everything to Goodwill. I recall that the associate at Goodwill asked if we were moving into a new house, to which we responded, "No." We then informed the associate that we were moving out of state, and she asked if we had already secured a job in that state, to which we responded, "No." She then stated that you all had to be brave and have a lot of faith moving to an unknown state. Faith was demonstrated by our courageous decision to resign and relocate from a well-paying position as a quality control chemist in North Carolina to an unknown state. I applied to a trauma one hospital as a pharmacy intern despite having no prior pharmacy experience. I submitted my application in the morning and after that we went out for grocery shopping, we got back to the house in a couple of hours only to find out that a message was left on the voice message requesting an interview; I interviewed with the hospital and got that job. You will never know what lies ahead of you until you take a bold step and move forward. As you continue to make decisions about your life one at a time, things will begin to unfold one at a time. Don't put off making that decision; I know that sometimes it's hard and scary to take that next step, but I'll encourage you to do so right now. Imagine that you are on a tour of the zoo and are admiring all the wonderful animals. However, one of the tigers has escaped from its cave and is running toward you at 100 miles per hour. At this point, you know your life is over and are terrified of having to either surrender and serve as the tiger's dinner or fight back. You won't have time to think about your next action, but I am sure you will make the quickest decision to find ways to defend yourself. Life's obstacles are there to keep you from getting where you want to go, but you can overcome them and learn the lessons that each obstacle brings your way. Sometimes, you can learn from other people's mistakes and avoid the paths they took to make them. Don't settle for less than the best because you have what it takes to bravely face life and succeed.

5

It's never too late to start again

*What you have where you are is what you need
to become who you are.*

SOMETIMES LIFE IS FRUSTRATING because we tend to be chasing the things we do not have and forget to thank God for the things we do have. If you will take time to appreciate the gift of life, and the possessions God has granted you, you will be able to enjoy a fulfilling life and discover how a complex life can be lived simply. When God created you, he endowed you with everything you will ever need to become what he intended you to be. So quit fighting over the things you do not have, and rather use the things you do have to create the things you do not have.

When you sow an orange seed in the ground, the power of that seed to germinate and bring forth oranges is hidden within the seed itself and never outside its perimeter. That seed in the ground is well equipped with all it needs to generate fruit of its kind. The only factor that can facilitate the growth of that seed is you taking care of it. You can care for that seed by providing the right type of soil and periodic irrigation and watching over it to ensure that seed brings forth its fruits. The same is true of your potential to become the champion God created you to be. You have the dynamite within you ready to explode for you to accomplish your God-given purpose on earth. All you need to do is to acknowledge that potential within you, pay attention to that potential, and transform it into the champion you want to be.

Sitting at the same place doing the same thing and blaming everybody for your circumstances is never going to change anything, and adds more woes to your troubles. If you find yourself trapped by your circumstances, and those circumstances are not changing for the better, you can start by changing your attitude and begin to see things from a productive perspective. Anything you will ever achieve in life is dependent on your attitude. If nothing around you is changing for you to have a good perception about life, you can make the necessary adjustments to be a better you, and everything around will respond positively to accommodate that change. Thus, you change your attitude to change the things around you.

Change is particularly important to humans; it is the blueprint of life that signifies and differentiates living things from non-living things. Any living thing must respond to change to grow. Can you imagine giving birth to a baby who turns five years old, and that baby is not growing, crawling, or talking? This will be one of the odds in life and contradict the principle of a living organism. If you are human, then you are a living organism, and as an organism that is alive and not dead yet, you must respond to changes no matter who you are and the level of status you've attained in life. I remember my son Caleb came to me when he was five years old with a shirt he was wearing when he was three years old; he then said, "Daddy, my shirt has gotten smaller and wouldn't fit me anymore." I responded by saying, "Son it is not that the shirt has gotten smaller, but rather you have changed and gotten bigger than the shirt." This illustrates the fact that we as humans are always growing and you will never be a champion in life until you are ready to acknowledge change and outgrow your unchanging circumstances. Your unpleasant circumstances may seem constant, but variable is your response. What you totally have control over and can vary to overcome such circumstances is your attitude.

If you tame an eaglet (immature eagle) and limit it to living with chickens, it will not be long, and you will see that eagle fully loaded with potential yet living and acting just like a chicken and limiting its potential to fly up high in the sky. But if awareness should dawn on that eagle and it be reminded where it belongs, you will be surprised how far that eagle can soar if it should respond to changes and have a corresponding approach. You may be an eagle but brought up as a chicken, and may have been told by your mother, father, or the people around you that you can never achieve anything good in life regarding your age as of now. They might have told you it is too late to live the life you have been dreaming of. It is an error: it is never too late to start again; put yourself together and like the eagle change your attitude, test your flapping wings again, and you will discover your potential to attain great heights in life.

When people complained they cannot accomplish such and such a thing because they were too old, my immediate question to them was "How old is old?" Age is only a number, and at times it has nothing to do with maturity. We all advance in age, but not all of us mature to live up to the standards that correspond to our respective ages. Grow vertically by acknowledging, fellowshipping, and living right with God, and mature horizontally by living with the people around you and looking at things from their perspectives.

Moses could have missed his divine opportunity to deliver the children of Israel if he had considered himself too old to be a deliverer. According to Acts 7:23, 30, *"When Moses was forty years old, he decided to visit his own people, the Israelites. . . . After forty years had passed, an angel appeared to Moses in the flames of a burning bush in the desert near Mount Sinai."* As of the time Moses left Egypt, he was forty years old, and after forty years of departing Egypt God spoke to him about his assignment in delivering the Israelites. This indicates Moses was eighty years old when he was recruited into God's plan to deliver the Israelites. You might be thinking Moses was too old to embark on such a mission, yet he did and got the job done. Now that I have established the fact that Moses was eighty years old when he started his career as a deliverer, you have no excuse to fold up your arms and think that you cannot reach your goal by reason of your age. No one is too old to accomplish a dream.

Exodus 4:1–5 asserts:

> *Moses answered, "What if they do not believe me or listen to me and say, 'The Lord did not appear to you'?" Then the Lord said to him, "What is that in your hand?" "A staff," he replied. The Lord said, "Throw it on the ground" and it became a snake, and he ran from it. Then the Lord said to him, "Reach out your hand and take it by the tail." So, Moses reached out and took hold of the snake by the tail and it turned back into a staff in his hand. "This," said the Lord, "is so that they may believe that the Lord, the God of their fathers, the God of Abraham, the God of Isaac and the God of Jacob has appeared to you."*

I can imagine tons of "what ifs" going through the mind of Moses after God had told him he was going to be the deliverer. As a senior citizen, Moses might have been contemplating his age and abilities to deliver the Israelites. He might have said something like "Lord, why me? Why did you choose such an old man to deliver the Israelites when there are young, strong, and able men like Aaron and Joshua?" Moses might have had a legitimate reason to think that Pharaoh and his entourage would not believe him or listen to him because he was known to have killed an Egyptian and tried to escape Egypt for his life. I believe Moses might have presented legitimate cases to persuade God to bypass him: he does not have any communication skills degree to sweet-talk Pharaoh, and all he had was his walking stick (staff), but God was not interested in Moses's lack of skills or incapability. Instead, when Moses was in doubt of his capability, God asked Moses, "What is that in your hand?" God was interested in what Moses had and was willing to transform whatever Moses had into any skills Moses did not have that were necessary to expedite the delivery of the Israelites. To help Moses's doubts, God initially converted Moses's staff into a snake to persuade Pharaoh that God Almighty had appeared to

Moses and chose him as the mouthpiece in delivering the Israelites. God used the same common staff Moses had in his hand to part the Red Sea for the Israelites to journey on a dried land into their motherland. You have whatever it takes to become what God intended you to be; it is not beyond your reach, and quit looking for the extraordinary. Just take a step of faith in obedience to use the common things you do have or around you and God will take those common things to do extraordinary things in your life.

The Bible accounts in 1 Samuel 17:48–51:

> *As the Philistine moved closer to attack him, David ran quickly toward the battle line to meet him. Reaching into his bag and taking out a stone, he slung it and struck the Philistine on the forehead. The stone sank into his forehead, and he fell face down on the ground. So David triumphed over the Philistine with a sling and a stone; without a sword in his hand, he struck down the Philistine and killed him. David ran and stood over him. He took hold of the Philistine's sword and drew it from the scabbard. After he killed him, he cut off his head with the sword.*

David was a shepherd boy who attended to his father's sheep, fed, and guarded them. One major characteristic of shepherds is that they spend most of their time wandering around with their sheep and having little contact with people. Therefore, one can think of David as an inexperienced little boy with little or no skills in dealing with people. It is obvious that David would have missed his divine opportunity to defeat Goliath if he had thought the only way to have killed Goliath was to have been enlisted in the Israelite army and taught skills in fighting with armor and swords. As a shepherd boy all David had within his reach to fight Goliath were stones in his bag and a sling. Little did David know that mastering the most common things available to him was what was going to make him an extraordinary figure in the history of the Israelites. David used the stones and sling he had to defeat Goliath in order to obtain the sword he never had to cut off his head. I will encourage you to keep practicing the skills readily available to you now, and anything your hand may find to do, please do it with all your heart as if you are doing it unto the Lord. You may want to be the manager or supervisor in your institution, but you are just a common worker as of now and far from a managerial position. Wherever you may find yourself in the chain of commands can be a significant stepping stone to seeing your dream come true as a manager. All you have got to do is to keep preparing yourself for an uncommon favor as you faithfully and diligently discharge your duties because it is the unique way of handling things in the company that will make you stand out among your colleagues and present you to management for promotion. If you can faithfully serve with what you have where you are then you can have unprecedented favor to receive what you do not have where you are. At many times what you do not have does not matter; rather what matters most is how you use the things you do have to achieve the things you do not have.

What God has spoken concerning your destiny is what is keeping you alive and protected.

The fact that you are still alive in this world is enough evidence to convince you that God is not done with you yet. God is shaping your life every moment by moment and getting you gradually toward every decent work he has prepared for you. It can sometimes be very painful in those preparatory moments, and it may seem that God has forgotten you and delayed your accomplishments. But remember your timings are in God's hands and not in your own hands, his ways are not your ways, and in his own designated time he will make all things beautiful in your life. Sometimes you may be tempted to think that your time to show up and bless the world with your divine talent is over or too late according to marathon disappointments you may have encountered. That's okay, because as humans such thoughts are bound to cross our minds sometimes, but you can be assured that God is never late or too early in your life, he is just on time to fulfill any promise he has made concerning your life, and your disappointments with men can actually be turned into an appointment with

God. Nothing in your life is over until you take your last breath as God commands your departure from this world. Until then, God will continue to use you upon your availability to him rather than your abilities to accomplish every single word he has spoken concerning your destiny regardless of your age, sex, or race. The reason you are not dead is not because of your handsomeness, not because of your beauty, or intelligence, it is because God has a plan on his timetable concerning you to be alive and do the things you are doing as of now.

The Scripture says in 1 Thess 5:24, *"The one who calls you is faithful, and he will do it."* If God has a purpose for you in the year 2050, the same God is faithful to keep his promise and preserve your life until that mission is accomplished. Until that year 2050 nothing can cut short your life simply because God has assigned you a duty to perform in that year. I have experienced three motor vehicle accidents and God kept me alive from all such terrible accidents. It was one sunny Sunday returning home after church service in the front seat of a taxi when the taxi collided with another vehicle. My right foot got trapped by a metallic plate upon the impact. As rescuers rallied to rescue me, they tried pulling me out of the car but were not successful in doing that because my foot was trapped. The harder the rescuers pulled me from the car, the deeper the plate cut through my ankle, and the faster my blood gushed out. I was finally rescued and rushed to the emergency room where I gradually recovered. The car I was riding in was damaged beyond repairs and the police report indicated that there was no way the passenger (me) in the front seat would have survived the accident, but I did. When I became conscious, I was given crutches, and the doctor said my feet were saved by the connecting tendons from my ankle, but my veins were damaged, and I might not be able to walk on my right leg again upon recovery. When I heard those words from the doctor something within me said, "Will you believe the report of the medical doctor or the report of the Lord?" Right then without any hesitation I refused to use the crutches and said, "I will walk on that leg again" and felt faith rising within me that God would heal me and make me whole. By the faithful prayers of my sister Florence, her husband, and all loved ones, I was made whole, and today I live to testify the grace and faithfulness of God. I am not just walking on that leg, but I have been running several miles six days a week every morning. If I had died in that accident, I would not have been alive to marry my wife Harriet, the beautiful queen of my castle to bring forth our charming, precious children, Caleb, Michaela, Joshua, and Madison. God knew he would need the service of these children to influence their generation, so he preserved Harriet's life and that of mine and allowed us to cross each other's path to fulfill that chapter of our lives. God also preserved and protected me to be alive because this book had not yet been written on the day of the accident. God spared my life to accomplish another chapter of my life by authoring this life-changing book according to his timetable concerning my life. The message that was preached on that Sunday morning just before the accident would surprise you. On that particular day, Dr. Mensa Otabil gave a sermon at the International Central Gospel Church on 2 Cor 4:8–10, *"We are hard pressed on every side, but not crushed; perplexed, but not in despair; persecuted, but not abandoned; struck down, but not destroyed. We always carry around in our body the death of Jesus, so that the life of Jesus may also be revealed in our body."* Tell me if this is a coincidence that the message came at the same time as the accident. I call it the supernatural occurrence, favor of God, and how God can prepare you ahead of things before they happen. The fact that I was struck down but not destroyed was a clear sign and assurance of God's promise to me that I would live to proclaim his goodness and complete my task. I am happy to announce to you that you were born with a purpose and a sense of discrete direction to fulfill that purpose. God has attached certain tasks to your name to be completed by you at a particular time in your life. No one else can perform those tasks better than you, regardless of your age. Nobody can take away your life until such tasks have been fulfilled. So, activate that faith and accomplish that dream. When Martin Luther King Jr. was alive, he showed up as an influential civil rights activist. When Mother Teresa was alive, she showed up and was known for her love. When Nelson Mandela was alive, he showed up opposing apartheid. You are still alive and existing, but have you shown up yet? It is your turn to show up; the world is waiting for your contributions.

6

From prison to prominence

Behind bars does not necessarily imply a wasted life; rather, it provides you with a second chance to act in accordance with the truth but in opposition to the verdict.

RENEWING YOUR MIND IS necessary if you want to overcome obstacles in life and rise to higher status. Your mind is like a computer database: whatever you hope to achieve in your life now or in the future will be a true reflection of what you feed it now. If you feed your mind good things, you will live to enjoy them. According to Rom 12:2, *"Do not conform to the pattern of this world, but be transformed by the renewing of your mind. Then you will be able to test and approve what God's will is—his good, pleasing and perfect will."* You have what it takes to advance from prison to the palace, from mediocre to a higher status, or from once a failure to a lifetime champion. It is acceptable that you have encountered some terrible setbacks in your life, and acceptable to fail at times in one's life, but it is never acceptable to remain a failure. Failures have the potential to ensnare you in a state of fear and stifle your desire to achieve success if you do not properly deal with them. To move forward in life, it is sometimes worth going back with a fresh mindset to confront and overcome those failures. Understanding those failures will enable you to break the patterns that led to them and give you the chance to try something new for a different result. Though he failed multiple times before succeeding, Thomas Edison was the most famous inventor of the light bulb. He interpreted his failures as a series of approaches that would not result in electric bulbs. How do you view your failures? I challenge you to think of your failures as a way to get closer to success rather than a destination you've reached. Before succeeding, Abraham Lincoln experienced several failures. Abraham Lincoln was defeated for state legislature in 1832, suffered the death of his wife in 1835, suffered a nervous breakdown in 1836, was denied the position of speaker in 1838, rejected for land officer in 1849, was defeated for US senate in 1854, was defeated again in his bid for the US senate in 1858, but in 1860 Abraham Lincoln, the die-hard man who was hungry and thirsty for success, was elected the sixteenth president of the United States of America. Do not give up; failures have no power over you; instead, use failure as a chance to successfully eliminate distractions and persevere until you succeed.

You may find yourself in a tight corner, or your life may seem to be wasted away because of a wrong decision you might have made. This wrong decision might have cost you important relationships in your life and might have compromised your integrity, making you think that your messed up situation will never get better. Wrong focus; God can take your mess and turn it into something meaningful to confound the people that might be thinking your life is so messed up that it can never be repaired. No mess or wasted life is beyond God's mercy. You can get back your life if you can rethink your thoughts. The Bible encourages us to renew our minds in order to obtain things that are different from what we might have already had or things better than what we have. If you can imagine how big God is, then you will understand how small your problem is. If you are at a low point in your life and the darkness is so dense that you can't see a way out, just remember to focus on how great your God is and how he can do anything to gradually lead you to understand that the darkness is only there to reveal your brightness and shine once more. A common proverb states, "You are as old as you think you are," and the same is true of your capacity to achieve anything you set out to do.

Being physically or mentally imprisoned entails restriction and confinement to a predetermined setting. One's ability to influence his or her surrounding environment outside of this setting is limited. In accordance with the rules of such a prison, one will be instructed on what to do, when to do it, and how to do it. The only thing you can control, though, is your internal environment. You have complete control over how you would like to regulate your feelings, emotions, thoughts, and behavior in this internal environment. You decide what to think, what to entertain, what to say, how to say it, when to say it, and how to behave. So, stop blaming everybody around you and take responsibility for maintaining sanity in your internal climate that only you have complete control. Get rid of the negative thoughts you've been having in the past and focus on moving forward. You should also surround yourself with the right group of people who will inspire you to succeed. I will challenge you to ask yourself one straightforward question: How can I make a positive impact on the people in my immediate environment right now? If the president should send a message to pardon one inmate at your camp, would you be the only prisoner at your camp who would receive a pardon from the president for good behavior and readiness to rejoin the free world? If the answer is no, then start making positive changes in your life right now and be prepared for opportunities that come your way. Make the most of the opportunity presented by all the lessons you have been receiving within this wall and put them to use for a better version of yourself. My career in prison ministry began with wonderful individuals like Skip Moseley, Steve Suits, John Bate, Joe Lenna, and Chris Olha, all of whom worked tirelessly to ensure the success of inmates. John, our guitarist, would occasionally request a day pass for a prisoner to eat lunch with them in an effort to assist them in reintegrating into society. Skip is a humble, selfless individual who loves the Lord dearly and will always offer to pick up our group to ride in his limousine to a minimum-security prison, where one of us will speak. Despite our individual differences, we worked well together to bring the best out of the inmates. Chaplain Joe Lenna introduced me to the prison ministry and helped me serve in the prison ministry at Caswell Correctional Center. Joe Lenna always reminds inmates to pray for their children because no one else will if they don't. Without waiting to be released from prison, you can easily incorporate this piece of advice into your daily prayers to see how your prayers can alter the situation and keep your family better prepared for your release. Chris Olha always enjoys sharing life-changing lessons with the inmates and encouraging them to apply biblical principles to have a personal encounter with God and complete their God-given task while they are in prison. For me, I share my life story and reassure the inmates that if God can get me this far, he can do the same for them if they stay in the environment of God's word. I always challenged them to live their best life and pray that their camp would one day be a good place to send inmates for reformation and that they should always set themselves apart for God's use and never be ashamed of the gospel.

Forgiveness is one sign of rising above one's circumstances. But you must first forgive yourself for any wrongdoing as well as the people who hurt you, never harboring resentment. The longer you hold a grudge, the more irrational you become and the more difficult it is to let go and allow God into your life. Other people may have hurt you so much that you have no reason to forgive them and will never forgive them as long as you live. Find a reason to forgive them because doing so helps you grow as a person and gets you ready for the next stage of your life. Jesus Christ died for you even though you were a sinner. He showed you mercy for your mess, gave you hope for your hopelessness, gave you grace for your impatience, showed you favor despite not being worthy of his glory, and was crucified for your sins. If Christ forgave you despite all these wrongdoings, then pay it forward, go and forgive those who hurt you to rebuild relationships and move on.

Had Joseph not forgiven his accusers when lied about, and his brothers when mistreated and traded away to foreigners, he would have never rise from prison to the palace. According to Gen 37:3–5, *"Now Israel loved Joseph more than any of his other sons, because he had been born to him in his old age; and he made an ornate robe for him. When his brothers saw that their father loved him more than any of them, they hated him and could not speak a kind word to him. Joseph had a dream, and when he told it to his brothers, they hated him all the more."* First, Joseph was hated for the simple reason that he was born to a father at an older age of which he had no control. Even though he was not to be blamed, his brothers disliked him and mistreated him. Second, his dream got him into trouble, made him more despised, and he ended up being sold into slavery. When he had the opportunity, Joseph had every reason to pay back with vengeance on his family, but instead, he forgave them and rescued them from the drought. Will you take vengeance or forgive your trespassers? Will you seek vengeance with resentment, or will you take the high road of forgiveness? The first step in Joseph's healing process from his mistreatment was forgiving his brothers. You will have peace of mind and be able to rise to new heights if you forgive those who have wronged you.

Integrity was another hallmark of Joseph's success in rising from prison to prominence. According to the book of Gen 39:6–12:

> *So Potiphar left everything he had in Joseph's care; with Joseph in charge, he did not concern himself with anything except the food he ate. Now Joseph was well-built and handsome, and after a while his master's wife took notice of Joseph and said, "Come to bed with me!" But he refused. "With me in charge," he told her, "my master does not concern himself with anything in the house; everything he owns he has entrusted to my care. No one is greater in this house than I am. My master has withheld nothing from me except you, because you are his wife. How then could I do such a wicked thing and sin against God?" And though she spoke to Joseph day after day, he refused to go to bed with her or even be with her. One day he went into the house to attend to his duties, and none of the household servants was inside. She caught him by his cloak and said, "Come to bed with me!" But he left his cloak in her hand and ran out of the house.*

Despite being in command of the pharaoh's entire household, Joseph was not arrogant and maintained his integrity. When the opportunity arises, you may view it as a chance to have a sexual encounter or flirt with your friend's or your master's wife. After all, you'll say, "I didn't ask for her, but she proposed to have an affair with me." Wrong focus; the fact that she presented herself to you does not mean that it is right. Even when no one was looking, Joseph maintained his integrity, did the right thing, and fled the scene. He was imprisoned for a crime he did not commit because Potiphar's wife lied about him and claimed he tried to rape her. He went to prison without harboring any grudges and diligently served his sentence, trusting that everything would be okay if he kept his integrity and did the right thing. If you take a moment to trade places with Joseph, you will discover that the situation was extremely challenging and that it will require an ordinary person with extraordinary determination, a keen sense of purpose, and a thirst for integrity. Be the bigger person and do the right thing even when no one is watching. Joseph established standards to help him achieve his goal of reaching the top one day. He upheld integrity as one of his fundamental values regardless of the odds against him. Set some unwavering, attainable goals that will propel you to prominence. These goals will necessitate minute mental adjustments that have the potential to significantly alter your life and the lives of those around you. If you are physically imprisoned for, say, ten years, that's a good ten years in solitary confinement, ten years without spending Christmas or Thanksgiving with your family, ten years without sharing your goals with them, and ten years without actively being involved in the lives of those you love and cheering on your children's accomplishments. It is difficult to state this but let me be honest and call a spade a spade rather than a big spoon: depending on your sentence, some of you will not escape prison alive. Please do not say that "when I get out of prison, my life will be different." Instead, live like there is not tomorrow and you only have today to make your life count. Contrary to your verdict, start making those changes now and live your best life now and every day. Imagine becoming the best version of yourself and having an impact on those around you. Before you know it, your fellow inmates will be asking you for life-changing advice and will have the chance to tell your story while incarcerated.

7

Character creates champions

Champions are destined to win. Winners must be prepared to win, and their character will guarantee future victories.

IF I HAVE ONE word to say before I depart from this world, it will be the nine-letter word *character*. This is because everything you ever owned or needed to maintain your status in life is going to depend on your character. Character is the prized possession of all the qualities a person may have that make them distinct from other people.

Destroy your character, and you will destroy your career! You might graduate from high school or college next week, next month, or next year. You might also start a new career, marry your spouse, start a new job, or get promoted at work. What an accomplishment! However, the quality of your character is the only thing that can keep this achievement going. You should not be different when you get home from school from what you were in the classroom. When you are all by yourself at your computer at 2 a.m., what you watch during the day when everyone else is around you should not be different from what you watch at 2 a.m. when no one else is around you. Our public lives should not be different from our private lives. Your no out in the open ought to be your no in privacy too. We must establish stringent guidelines that will enable us to live our own lives and prevent us from living like everyone else because the kind of life you live today will determine the level of success you will have tomorrow. Your character is trapped in your day-to-day activities. How you respond to situations at home and school is exactly how you will be responding to situations at work. Therefore, take some time to work on yourself daily. You cannot change all the people in your immediate environment. However, you can change and improve yourself. Instead of focusing on how to become a better person, many of us spend our lives worrying about how others will judge us. Some of the people in your life will initially like you, but they will come to dislike you over time. Some will despise you at first yet are going to adjust their perspectives and like you. Others will like you regardless of anything; regardless of whether you dishearten them they will in any case remain with you. You will never be liked by other people, no matter what! But that is okay; focus on yourself and do your best. Your own opinion, not the opinion of others, is the most important opinion. However, you need to be careful about the character you are building because what you do in the dark will one day become known. Character is like pregnancy; regardless of how hard you hide it, it will appear! People may not be sure whether you are pregnant or have gained some weight in the second or third trimester of your pregnancy. Yet, on the seventh to eighth months, it becomes clear that you are pregnant, and all doubts will be cleared; this is how character may be depicted. If you are the kind of person who will always tell people what you think at anytime and anywhere behaving like a chameleon, tomorrow will come and your betrayed character will leave you lonely without any friends or support.

If you ever forget anything, please do not forget your humble beginnings. It is in the humble beginnings where one's belief systems are rooted by one's parents or guardians; this is when parents help us to form our belief system to differentiate standards between what is morally acceptable and unacceptable. Character begins at home. I am the last born of eight siblings and growing up in a Christian environment my mother's rule of the house was if you chose not to go to church on Sunday then you chose not to eat until everybody was home after church. As much as it seemed like torture then when I was young, I now wish my parents were here to thank them for instilling these practical values in me. The lesson behind no church, no food was never to punish us but to teach us to have a heart of appreciation to God who watches over us, protects, and provides for us throughout the week and I needed to give at least two hours of my Sunday to him. Thinking about it now is not a bad training at all, going to church for couple of hours on a Sunday for an exchange of knowledge to enhance my character to live right for a better me, because no Bible-believing church will teach you to deform in character. It was difficult keeping up with going to church every Sunday, but with time it became easier and I began looking forward to Sunday services as these biblical teachings I learnt at church strengthened and gave me a solid foundation for a character I can be proud of.

"Thou shalt not lie" was the most important household rule for my mother. My mom's brilliant rule at home was to come clean regardless of what the outcomes were. Although it may be painful telling the truth now, it will prevent several scars that will last a lifetime. A mark of honor that forms the foundation of a strong character that will help shape society in a positive way is instilling in us the value of upholding the truth and avoiding lies. Simply envision how silly you will look when over and over you denied reality and eventually came to spotlight that you did what you said you did not do. You lose credibility and betray trust when this happens. The pregnancy model illustrates that while the truth lasts indefinitely, lies cannot. It is analogous to covering a Styrofoam container with layers of materials to sink it to the ocean's bottom; however, as the materials wear away, the container will eventually rise to the surface of the water and be visible to all. The same is true for lying; if you tell a simple lie, you will need to cover it up with more lies that are bigger than the first one, and you will keep adding increasingly bigger lies for coverage. If you tell a lie the first time, do not deny the truth the second time; come clean, resolve the issue, establish some safe guardrails, and move on. Eventually, those layers will fall and reveal the covered lies. As a result, my advice to you is not to attempt to tell one and you will not have to remember to defend it.

According to Prov 22:6, *"Start children off on the way they should go, and even when, they are old they will not turn from it."* The Bible commands us to train our children. We have a responsibility to raise our children to the highest possible standards and to train them in the right manner as parents or caregivers. Scripture instructs us to train them when they are still young. This is because it is simpler to train a child to become a responsible individual than it is to attempt to correct them when they are adults and have already established a negative outlook on life. Despite the fact that educators teaches our children in school, character is least taught in the classroom for our children to become responsible citizens, and it's an important mission at hand on parents to prepare their children at home prior to getting into the educational system, train them to be equipped yet not with weapons or swords but rather with truth to be strong and dedicated to protect truth and never bow to any strain to circumvent truth in school, work places, or any place they find themselves. Teach them to be disciplined soldiers who never let down their guard but instead remain focused and faithful in their interactions with humanity. Teach them to always consider things from God's perspective and to be good stewards of life. This is because God is all-knowing and all-powerful, and we would never make a mistake if we followed his instructions and did what he said. Training our children to have the right point of view in life will not just assist them with understanding others, yet additionally it will set them apart to succeed and turn out to be less stressful than their counterparts who do not place things in their right perspectives. Having the right perception increases the rate at which you quickly identify your talent and live a purposeful life. If you live your life with a purpose, you will not waste time in a way that does not help you get where you are going in life. One might ask, "How would you identify your assignment in life?" In addition, I would like to follow up with a second question: "What is it that keeps you up at night that you excel at?" It really is not hard: just figure out what keeps you awake and what you are passionate about, do the things you are passionate about, incorporate them into your daily routine, do them consistently, reevaluate, and improve after each assessment until your good becomes better and your best is achieved.

I am always looking for positive ways to impact or be impacted by other people. I try to educate my pharmacy technicians, fellow pharmacists, learners, and other healthcare professionals on a particular topic by creating a section at work called "teachable moments with Stephen." In these sections, I explain in detail the reasons behind what we do. The team works efficiently to achieve goals and becomes compliant with the company's policies and procedures. Once understanding is clarified, enthusiasm to work is motivated and employees become less disagreeable and work with minimum supervision. The same is true for our children; when we teach them the right way to do things and help them understand why they should do what they should, they can easily do the right things without having to worry about questioning their choices. It is one thing to tell your children what to do; it is another to take the time to explain things to them and help them understand, and understanding is what helps build a formidable character. Coming from an African household, our parents always told us not to drink or smoke because you will die if you do. They are on the right path, yet consider the possibility that I did drink and smoke and did not die; at that point, I will consider them to be liars and do something contrary to anything they tell me going forward. However, they are right, and their points would be well received if they took the time to research and inform us about the dangers of smoking and drinking, as well as the likelihood of death. This is because if you take the time to educate your children about life and the possible outcomes of their choices, they are more likely to believe you. They might not do what you asked of them yet, assuming the adverse result of their contrary activity happened, they will begin to accept you and say, "Mother or father told me so," and they are correct. As much as you can, please teach your children to understand the why to achieve the goal. In all your getting, get understanding.

Character is simply commitment! You are committed to behaving in a certain manner and expect a particular outcome. If you take the time today to do the uncommon things common people will not do, then you will receive the uncommon things common people will not have tomorrow. Do not behave like anybody else and start with small commitments. For example, you are in traffic and running late to work or school. You may be tempted to get angry at the red light and start cursing the driver ahead of you driving slowly. Just pause and ask yourself if this is a battle worth fighting? You will realize it is not! Instead go with the flow and say to yourself that this delay may be preventing me from an accident ahead, so I am going to keep my cool and enjoy some praise music or podcast. You are getting late to a function and could not find your car key and getting tensed up and about to unload your frustrations on your kids or spouse; pause and ask if this is a battle worth fighting—it is not; change your attitude and rather call your kids and spouse to help you find the keys, and this will be done faster and in a friendly environment. This smaller habit formation will tend to be the foundation for a solid character. If there is anything missing in our society, it will be character, and your character will be tested by the challenges we encounter. Great men and women, leaders in high positions, have fallen because their characters were tested and found vulnerable, so build a quality character today so you can enjoy its benefits tomorrow.

8

Life is short, live

The people around you serve as bridges to your future.

LIFE IS LIKE A puzzle; it is unfinished until every one of the pieces are assembled. Consider that you are trying to fit the parts of an alligator puzzle together one at a time. When two or three of the components are put together, possibly starting with the tail end, the tail will resemble any other tail and it will be impossible to distinguish from closely related animals like the crocodile. However, as one carefully goes on to discover the remaining parts and fit them together, the overall picture starts to resemble an alligator in some way. However, the picture will not be finished until the last piece is in place, and that will set the alligator apart from other creatures. Until you discover and fulfill the purpose for which you were born, life is not complete. It is not a destiny or a finished product; rather, it is a work in progress that must be taken one step at a time in accordance with God's word.

We are tightly knitted together in this world to complement one another. To make life work, we need each other's support and encouragement. Nobody has ever achieved a particular social status or material wealth without the assistance of others. All the people we meet throughout our lives are orchestrated by God, not by chance or just by chance. In a short amount of time, you will comprehend why you met this person at that point in your life to save you or assist with a need. Because you never know who is connected to your divine destiny, take the time to appreciate the people in your life and treat them with respect.

Who knows what significant part of your life your neighbor might play? Who is aware of the divine connection that exists between you, your assistant, coworkers, friends, or even the person seated next to you at church, on a bus, or on a flight? Who is aware of that child? Do you think you know your child, parents? You do not really know that child very well. You only see him or her as a normal child or as a naughty child who only causes you trouble. However, that child has a lot of potential that will blow your mind if you love, train, and treat him or her right.

The Bible reveals a divine connection between Naaman and his servant girl. Second Kings 5:1–3 accounts:

> *Now Naaman was commander of the army of the king of Aram. He was a great man in the sight of his master and highly regarded, because through him the LORD had given victory to Aram. He was a valiant soldier, but he had leprosy. Now bands from Aram had gone out and had taken captive a young girl from Israel, and she served Naaman's wife. She said to her mistress, "If only my master would see the prophet who is in Samaria! He would cure him of his leprosy."*

Syria's general was Naaman; he was a hero who was respected for his bravery in leading the Syrian army to victory in numerous conflicts. If Naaman somehow managed to be in our contemporary world, Naaman would have been perceived as the second in command in his country, and you can envision him being brightened with gold, decorations, and extraordinary honors as a valiant fighter. However, he was a leper and needed assistance for healing.

The Syrians took Israeli captives and brought them to Syria during one of the Syrian victories over the Israelites. A young girl taken as a slave for Naaman's wife was one of the captives. The key to Naaman's healing was linked to this innocent little foreign girl. She told Naaman's wife that Israel had a prophet who can cure her husband of leprosy. After listening to his servant girl, obeying the prophet Elisha, and immersing himself seven times in the Jordan River, Naaman's flesh was restored and made whole. Naaman, his family, and the entire Syrian army had no idea that a captive they had taken from the war could reversibly save their general. This little girl might not have had the courage to suggest a solution to her master's predicament if Naaman had mistreated her and restricted her to the kitchen, laundry, housework, and scrubbing bathrooms and toilets. Additionally, if Naaman had denied her the right to sit at the same table as his nuclear family, the little girl might not have been able to suggest a solution to her master's predicament. There is a proverb that states that the people you encounter when climbing up are the same people you will meet when descending, so treat everybody around you right. Sometimes it may be very tempting to lose hope and get tired of treating people right when they do not recognize and appreciate your good efforts, but rather criticize and reciprocate your good efforts with envy. That is okay; no matter what you do in life there are some people who will never appreciate your good works. Do not kill yourself for those people, but remember God created you to do what is right and not to please everybody in the world. If you try to please and make everyone happy, the only person who will not be pleased or happy is YOU. Do all you can in your power to be at peace with everybody, but if some people continue to prove that they do not want you around them, do not pity yourself and beat yourself down. Rather, keep living right and doing the right things because you might be inspiring somebody else somewhere who is somehow watching, and appreciating your life. Do not lose heart doing the right things even when wrong things are happening to you.

Life is too short to waste today dwelling on yesterday's resentment when you can make the most of today to brighten tomorrow.

Life is too short to be wasted, and the next second of your life is not guaranteed. I used to have severe stomach pain most often when I was in Ghana; it would get so agonizing that I bent down and stopped walking to catch my breath, and whenever it happened and I went to the emergency clinic, they generally took it lightly and treated me for common abdominal pain and sent me home. When I first came to the United States and was living with my sister Nellie in Rochester, New York, Nellie took me out to see two or three Ghanaians in the area. We met one of her Ghanaian companions where we had dinner together at his home. Following dinner, I began having severe stomach pain and was rushed to the nearest emergency hospital, which was a couple of minutes away from where we had the dinner. They treated me for abdominal pain and were going to release me once I felt alright. Nonetheless, Nellie demanded and stated that she would not bring me back home until they truly stabilized me. I was ready to leave and impatient with Nellie and told her, "I'm okay and not hurting any longer." Nonetheless, Nellie wouldn't budge and kept on advocating on my behalf. It was not long before I began having severe abdominal pain again and this time I began crying that I was losing my breath; they rushed me to do abdominal X-ray, and the X-ray was negative for masses or holes in my digestion tracts. As I was on the stretcher being pushed back to my room to be discharged, I felt a similar sharp, severe stomach pain and was hurried again for stomach X-rays, and this time the X-ray showed a perforated duodenum, and they needed to perform emergency medical surgery. The surgeon was gone for the day and had left the hospital. However, they paged him, and he turned around to return to the emergency clinic for the urgent medical procedure. I was prepared for the surgery, and a surgery that should have gone on for two hours went on for five hours. When surgery was over, the surgeon told me I was lucky and that if things were a bit delayed my life would have been wasted. The surgeon said I was lucky, but I will say God's grace and mercy saved me. What are the odds that I visited the United States at that time, ate food that upset my stomach so bad to end up at the emergency room, and that Nellie's friend's house was just a couple of minutes from the hospital for that urgent surgery to be performed to save my life. Nothing occurs coincidentally; whatever you are going through, God has a way of preserving you and turning your situation into something purposeful. God is never too late or too early; he is dependable and always on time to execute his plan for your life, and however short life seems to be it merits carrying on with your life for God.

In this book, I try to encourage you to live life fully and enjoy your life because life is too short to be wasted. According to Ps 90:10, *"Our days may come to seventy years, or eighty, if our strength endures; yet the best of them are but trouble and sorrow, for they quickly pass, and we fly away."* God has granted that if all things being equal, we should live up to 70 years or over. You might be thinking that 70 years is limitless, and it will consume a huge chunk of time to arrive at that age. You got it all wrong; it is not as long as you think. I will take my time to illustrate to you how short life is. Now, let us perform some straightforward mathematics here by converting the 70 years into months, the months into weeks, and finally the weeks into days. Three hundred and sixty-five days (about 12 months) makes 1 year. This implies out of the 70 years, you have 25,550 (70 x 365) days to live. This figure is even less than someone's bank account. Thus, your number of days on earth is someone's bank account; it is too short, isn't it? Get a piece of paper and write down your present age for me to illustrate how short your life is as of now. Assuming you are 25 years old, this will mean that you have spent 9,125 (25 x 365) days of your life already. Twenty-five years of your life is gone, and you now have 45 (70–25) years to live. Forty-five years of your life is equivalent to 16,425 (25,550–9,125) days. Thus, you only have 16,425 days remaining for you to live and leave the world better than you found it. Let us continue to break things down into simpler forms as detailed below:

- Converting 70 years to hours:
    - 70 x 365 x 24 = 613,200 hours
    - How many years do you actively work in your entire life?
        - » Early retirement age = 62 years
        - » Working age = 16 years
        - » Active working years = 62–16 = 46 years
        - » 1 year = 52 weeks

- You work 40 hours per week, assuming no vacation:
  - 40 x 52 = 2,080 hours/year
    - Thus, in a year you will work 2,080 hours
  - 2,080 hours x 46 active working years = 95,680 hours
    - Thus, in your entire life you will actively work 95,680 hours
- How many hours are in a year?
  - 365 days x 24 hours = 8,760
    - Thus, you have 8,760 hours in a year
  - Therefore, 95,680 active working hours/8,760 = 10.9 (~11) years
    - Thus, in your entire life you will actively work for 11 years

- How many hours do you sleep in your entire life?
  - According to the National Sleep Foundation, an adult needs about 8 hours of sleep per day
  - 8 hours x 365 = 2,920 hours/year x 70 years = 204,400 hours
  - Thus, if you live for 70 years and sleep 8 hours/day, then in 70 years you will sleep 204,400 hours
  - 204,400/8,760 = 23.33 (~ 23) years
    - Thus, for 70 years of your life, you sleep 23 years
- How many hours of TV do you watch in your entire life?
  - According to the United States Department of Labor, Bureau of Labor statistics conducted in 2017:
    - Average hours spent per day by Americans watching TV is 2.8 hours
    - 2.8 x 365 x 70 = 71,540 hours
    - 71,540/8,760 = 8.2 (~8) years

- Thus, at 70 years of age, 8 years of the life of an average American will be attributed to watching television.

Totaling these selected few (active working years, sleep years, and TV years) results in 11+23+8 = 42 years. Now going back to the simple assessment of writing down your age, subtract 42 years from the number of years remaining for you to live. Again, assuming you are 25 years old, in this case 25 years of your life are gone, and you only have 45 years (70–25) remaining if you should live up to 70 years. Subtract 42 years from the remaining years and you will be shocked to see that you are either in the negatives, owing life or having very few years to make life work. In this case, 45–42 = 3 years. Thus, if you are 25 years old as of now then you have 3 years to put your life together. However, it is unfortunate that the years you have left to live are also filled with uncertainties. For instance, the unpredictable factors that are also working against your few remaining days on this planet include difficulties, sorrows, illnesses, failures, and accidents. This demonstrates how short your life is, so take advantage of it while you can. According to Luke 3:23, *"Now Jesus himself was about 30 years old when he began his ministry."* Jesus did not live longer in years; however, the content of his life is so rich that it fills pages of the Bible and he continues to serve as the savior, leader, and a character to emulate. He lived for about 32–33 years and did not begin his public ministry until 30. You are never too old to begin the life that was meant for you. On the other hand, Methuselah was the only human being who lived the longest according to Gen 5:27: *"Altogether, Methuselah lived a total of 969 years, and then he died."* Even though Methuselah lived for 969 years, not much was said about him other than that he died. Is that how you would like your story to end? Instead of focusing solely on numbers, begin living a life of content. *You no longer need to waste any seconds*; start making decisions that will change your life and improve it right away. Let us go an extra mile and convert the 70 years into hours, hours into minutes, and finally minutes into seconds. Twenty-four hours makes 1 day. Consequently, the number of hours in a year is 8,760 (365 x 24) hours. One hour is equivalent to 60 minutes, and 1 minute is equivalent to 60 seconds. As a result, the number of seconds in a year is 31,536,000 (8,760 x 60 x 60). We now multiply the number of seconds per year by 70 to obtain the number of seconds in 70 years. Thus, 31,536,000 x 70 = 2,207,520,000 seconds. This indicates that we have approximately 2,207,520,000 seconds left to live. Once again, this figure is significantly less than someone's bank account, indicating how short your life is when broken into simpler terms.

Now the scariest part is this: you have spent some time reading this book as of now, assuming you have spent one hour so far. That one hour is equivalent to 3,600 (1 x 60 x 60) seconds, and this implies that 3,600 seconds of your life are gone while reading this book. Therefore, let me make this profound statement that even as you are reading this life-changing book where you are now, you are slowly but surely dying as that clock continues to tick and those seconds pass by. Anytime God blesses you to wake up and witness another day in your life is an indication that you are one day closer to your grave, or one day less your total number of days on the earth. So why do you want to lash out at everyone and go about your day in anger? If possible, ask yourself: is this situation worth taking away my joy? It is not worth your happiness, so continue living joyfully and treat such circumstances as minor. Imagine you went to see your primary care physician and were informed you only have 6 months to live: who would you call? What would you say? What would you do differently? I am sure you would live each day like it is your last day on earth and take time to enjoy friends, family, and loved ones. Living in such a way and doing your best every day, paying attention to the things you do on a regular basis and doing them well with all your heart, is the key to success in life. At this moment when there is a wake-up call to how short life can be then you might be thinking, you must decide whether to remain in your present circumstances or go the extra mile to make your life a bit better. You are not enjoying your life fully because you are full of resentment, and cannot get over what your brother, sister, friend, or spouse did to you. Or perhaps, you looked into the dark days of your life and were never proud of the life you led. The first and immediate thing to do is to set yourself free by forgiving yourself. Quit looking into your past and blaming yourself for some of the wrong things you might have done. But look at your life today and forgive yourself, encourage yourself, surrender everything to God, and keep looking forward for a brighter future because your best moments are yet to come and never in your past.

To live a productive life, you must give up some control and allow God to intervene on your behalf. Be aware that the more you think about those who might have hurt you in some way, the angrier and more unforgiving you become. A life that is unforgiving eventually leads to pride, and pride will promote your destruction. You cannot enjoy your life fully because you are choked with all these people that are waiting for your forgiveness. It is just like waking up in the morning and thinking about all the people you have imprisoned in your heart instead of focusing on a strategic plan that may be essential to your day's success. You only have one heart, and if you have held all these captives in your heart, there will be absolutely no room to hold the things that are most enjoyable and pleasing to you. Like the Lord's Prayer: "Forgive us our debts, as we also have forgiven our debtors." We are urged by Jesus to daily practice forgiveness. For some of you, the only thing you need to do to regain your happiness and enjoy life is to truly forgive the person who may have caused you pain. Forgiveness carries so much joy and power. When you let go of your resentment, you automatically bring back your joy. Therefore, if you free those captives of your heart, and forgive them, you will undoubtedly experience God's peace.

9

Your word is your world

Be careful what you say because, like a bullet shot from a rifle, words out of your mouth cannot be reclaimed and have potential to help or hurt.

Words are things that we declare with our mouths that are not visible, yet are capable of influencing and dictating the course of our lives. If you want to have an idea of how your life will look in a year or two down the road, just pay attention to whatever words you are declaring now regarding your future, because the invisible words you are declaring today will become a visibly evident tomorrow when it has fully taken root.

The Bible asserts, according to Heb 11:3, *"By faith we understand that the universe was formed at God's command, so that what is seen was not made out of what was visible."* God created the world by speaking forth invisible words to bring forth visible creation. This points to the fact that if you don't have a word, then you do not have a world. Words are very powerful in creating a substantial life. For example, I believe you do not have any orange with you at this moment, but when I mention the word "orange," all your mental faculties adjust themselves to immediately create a mental picture of what an orange should look like. That shows the potency of a spoken word, so be careful of the words that you are speaking into your life now, as those words will surely manifest in your future. Are you speaking the words of a failure, such as "nothing good will ever happen to me in life"? Or speaking the words of a champion, such as "I can do all things through Christ who strengthens me"?

Some people are very skillful in using their words to vividly explain, giving tangible reasons for why they are in such a situation or why they should continue to remain in such a situation. I do agree with such eloquent people who can use choice words to convince everybody about their present circumstances. But I also believe that descriptive words are not adequate. Go beyond describing your circumstances and speak blessings and favors into your future.

Joel 3:10 declares, *"Beat your plowshares into swords, and your pruning hook into spears: let the weakling say, 'I am strong!'"* "Let the weak say, I am strong" is a biblical principle that entreats us to declare words that are reflective of how we want our lives to look like in the future, rather than pity partying in our present circumstances. Today, you might be weak, but do not spend all your time talking about your weaknesses. Talk about the unprecedented strength that God is bringing your way; keep expecting it and it shall surely be yours for an inheritance.

As short as our lives may be on this planet, you do not want to waste any more time sitting in one place giving a discrete description of your present unfulfilling life. Rather, begin to declare things in your favor that will change your present unfulfilling situation, and use your imagination to envision where you want to be in the near future. When I was in high school, I would get excited any time I saw the seniors in the chemistry lab dressed up in their white lab coats. As I continue to admire those students in their lab coats, I began to say out loud to myself very frequently that I have what it takes to work in a science lab, and that I have made it through college, and have passed all my science classes. I constantly fed this passion and took the necessary steps to attain such ambition. Those positive declarations eventually took root, and I was successful in pursuing a science degree and becoming a quality control chemist. Any time I put on that lab coat at work, it reminds me of the declaration I made in the past. It happened to me; it can happen to you as well if you do not quit declaring and taking the steps necessary to achieve your ambition.

As stated in Isa 55:11, *"so is my word that goes out from my mouth: It will not return to me empty but will accomplish what I desire and achieve the purpose for which I sent it."* Any time God sends out his words, he expects that those spoken words have no choice but to manifest in the manner they were spoken and accomplish the required task for which they were sent forth. God treasures this principle so much that he said in Jeremiah that he knows the plans that he has for his children are plans to prosper them and give them a bright future. God does not have to wait for you to grow up and attain a particular status before he can tell you everything about your attained status. He can tell you everything about your future even when you were in your mother's womb. He already knew your end from your beginning. How? God knows your future because of the choice words he has declared in your favor. He remembers everything he has said concerning you, and those spoken words compel God to act in a manner that his actions will not contradict his spoken words.

As people created in God's own image, we have the potential to make declarations and watch over those declarations to see them happen in our lives. All you need to do is to speak out your words in faith in the direction you want your life to go; act in accordance with your declaration to ensure that your actions match your spoken words. This is especially important in keeping you in check of how to live your life and where to focus your strengths for the ultimate results. Also, when your words are similar to your actions, you will have enough control in making use of all available resources necessary to help you achieve your goal faster in life while eliminating or avoiding things that may waste your time. As a rule of thumb, send out your words today into your tomorrow, imagine your bright tomorrow, and start from your today to gradually attain your tomorrow in the direction of your spoken words.

In Matt 12:36–37, *"But I tell you that everyone will have to give account on the day of judgment for every empty word they have spoken. For by your words, you will be acquitted and by your words you will be condemned."* Jesus calls to our attention the importance of words. On the day of judgment when this world has ended and each of us is expected to give an account of our lives on earth, one thing stands clear: that each will be judged according to all the words one has spoken while alive. Thus, the word you are speaking now is the kind of world you are creating around yourself, and you will have to account for each spoken kind or careless word. So do yourself a great favor by considering every single word that comes out of your mouth. Be careful what you harbor in your heart because whatever is abundant in your heart is what your mouth will speak out. If you send forth unpleasant words, you will surely call forth unpleasant trouble. For that reason, send forth pleasant words to call forth a life that is most pleasing and rewarding.

About the Author

Growing up in Ghana can be difficult on its own, and especially where government assistance is scarce and frequently difficult to obtain, the loss of both parents can present significant challenges not limited to financial, emotional, and educational challenges.

Stephen lost his mother as a teenager. His mother was all he had at any point, and after losing his mother, his father took on full obligation of his life, but he likewise passed on about a year or so after his mom's death. Subsequently, Stephen lost two significant personalities in his life within a brief time frame. Stephen also lost his older brother during the same time frame as his dad. At this point, he was very worried and afraid of life, and he often thought about how unfair it was. Stephen walked around the streets of Ghana and people pointed fingers at him, feeling for him, and offering expressions like, "Because he didn't have a good start in life, I feel sorry for this boy. What else could have happened to him?" It continued forever, but Stephen's faith in God, on the other hand, steadily increased throughout all of these trying times, while his trust in people dramatically decreased. He began spending more time in prayer, studying and memorizing scriptures in the Bible, and in the long run turned out to be completely persuaded that if he could stay in the environment of God's word, God would take him to places he never dreamt of. Stephen made a major decision to never let tragedy or the loss of all the people he trusted with his life take away his joy. Those people once existed and contributed to his life in some way; however, their genes and footprints have been permanently wiped out from the planet's surface, and for that matter, Stephen put his faith in God and began to soar like an eagle. The joy of being in the Lord brought hope to him and gave him every reason to have a good success in all his endeavors. Today, Stephen is where he is because he took time to nurture that joy that comes from within. With perseverance Stephen became the first of eight siblings to attain a university degree to practice as a quality control chemist who developed and validated the High-Performance Liquid Chromatography to determine Chlorhexidine concentrations in lumen of epidural catheters within one year of hire at Teleflex Medical. Stephen furthered his education to earn a doctorate degree in pharmacy. Stephen is married to his beautiful wife, Harriet, and has four precious children, Caleb, Michaela, Joshua, and Madison. Stephen strongly believes that people can rob you of your money, tell lies on you, strip you of your garments and put you in prison, but they cannot take away your joy.

9 781666 785210